D1305440

First American edition 1998 by
Franklin Watts
A Division of Grolier Publishing
Sherman Turnpike
Danbury, CT 06816

Library of Congress Cataloging-in-Publication
Data
Pluckrose, Henry Arthur.
      On the farm / Henry Pluckrose : [illustrator, Teri
Gower].
           p. cm. -- (Machines at Work)
      Includes index.
      Summary: Photographs and simple text present
some of the different machines use don farms, including
tractors, cultivators, balers, and combine haarvesters.
      ISBN 0-531-14496-8 (lib. bdg.)   0-531-15352-5
(pbk.)
      1. Agricultural machinery--Juvernile literature. [1.
Agricultural machinery.   2. Machinery.] I. Gower, Teri, ill.
II. Title. III. Series: Pluckrose, Henry Arthur. Machines at
work.
S675.25.P58   1998
631.3--dc21   97-51398
                             CIP
                             AC

Printed in Belgium

Editor: Kyla Barber
Art Director: Robert Walster
Designer: Diane Thistlethwaite
Illustrator: Teri Gower

MACHINES AT WORK

On the Farm

Henry Pluckrose

FRANKLIN WATTS
A Division of Grolier Publishing
NEW YORK • LONDON • HONG KONG • SYDNEY
DANBURY, CONNECTICUT

Farmers grow food.
They also care for the animals
that give us meat, milk, and wool.
Farmers use many different
machines on the farm.

A tractor is a very useful machine.
The farmer uses the tractor
to push and pull other machines.

Before tractors were invented,
farmers used oxen, horses,
donkeys, or mules.

A dairy farmer keeps
cows for their milk.
The cows are milked
by machine.

The milk is loaded onto a truck
and taken away.

Some farmers keep sheep.
Sheep give us meat and wool.
Each sheep is sheared once a year.

The shepherd shears the sheep
with electric clippers.

Plants grow in the soil.
The farmer uses machines
to spread manure on the ground
and put goodness into the soil.

The machine being pulled
by the tractor is a slurry spreader.
Slurry is liquid manure from the
sheds where the cows and pigs live.

Seeds will not grow well
if the soil is too hard.

A plow pulled by a tractor
cuts through the hard soil.

The blades of the plow
break up the soil.

When the field has been plowed, the tractor pulls a cultivator across the ground to make the soil smooth.

Then the farmer uses a seed
drill to plant the seeds.

tractor

The seed drill
plants the seeds.

At the end of the summer,
the farmer cuts and harvests grass.
The grass is used
to feed the cows in winter.

baler

A machine cuts the grass
and packs it into bales.

The combine harvester is
the biggest machine on the farm.
It moves across the field
and cuts the wheat.

It also takes the grain off the stalk.

The farmer sits in the cab to
drive the combine harvester.

Sharp blades cut
the stalks.

Some farmers grow potatoes. Potatoes grow in the ground. Machines are used to plant and harvest potatoes.

The potato harvester lifts each potato plant from the soil.

The leaves are cut off the potatoes.

A moving belt carries the potatoes to a truck.

Once the crops are harvested,
the farmer prepares the field
for the next year.

milk lorry

Glossary

combine harvesters cut the wheat and take off the grain.

crops are plants grown by the farmer for food.

cultivators make the ground smooth.

harvest time is when the crops are collected.

seed drills plant the seeds in the soil.

tractors push and pull all the other machines.

plow and tractor

Index

seed drill